A Sunshine Garden Doll Pattern

Marigold

By Anne Cote

Marigold

Daisy

Sunflower

For more Sunshine Garden Dolls Patterns
Visit bluedaisyzone.com

Poppy

Dandelion

Marigold

Rosemary

Sage

Primrose

ISBN-13: 978-1-940354-62-0

Text, Photos, and Illustrations by Anne Cote
Cover Design by Anne Cote & Layne Walker
Edited by Joan Cote and Layne Walker

First edition published in August 2020
Published by New Friends Publishing, LLC
Lake Havasu City, AZ

Visit New Friends Publishing's Website at
www.newfriendspublishing.com

CONTENTS

To my sister
Joan Marie Cote,
who plants love and caring
along her path

Materials for Marigold

Marigold stands out with her fiery red hair and green eyes. Floral fabric with greens, yellows, and oranges bring out her coloring. Green hair ribbons and sash highlight her eyes. She is 20" tall.

SUPPLIES

There are lots of options for materials, including scraps of fabric and fancy trims. I've listed the products I use in brackets. Other options abound and are listed below.

DOLL

44"x13" cotton fabric for body [Lightweight Muslin]
Craft paint, markers, pastel stick
      [Anita's Shamrock mixed with one drop of Anita's
      Black for eyes; Anita's White for dots in the eyes]
      [Sharpie Permanent Markers for nose, brows, lashes,
      mouth]
      [Red/Orange pastel stick for cheeks]
Yarn for hair [Yarn Bee Fireside "Mandarin"]
Poly-fil Stuffing 6-8 oz.
Stuffing tools [tube and stick]
Fabric turning tools [tube and stick, see instructions]

CLOTHING

44"x19" cotton floral fabric for dress and bloomers
16"x4" cotton solid fabric for sash
20"x4" cotton solid fabric for hair bows
12"x8" black felt for shoes

31" ¾"-1" lace trim (flat or gathered) for dress skirt
18" ¾"-1" lace trim (flat or gathered) for bloomers
11" ¾"-1" lace trim (flat or gathered) for neckline
      (Total trim lace: 60")

8" 1/4" elastic for sleeves
9" 1/4" elastic for bloomers
2 snap fasteners
General sewing supplies

OPTIONS

Face can be painted, embroidered, or drawn on with permanent markers.
Cheek blush can be made with powdered blush or chalks.
Bloomers in a contrasting color require a 20"x10" piece of fabric. Dress still takes 44"x18" without the bloomers.
Hair may require more or less strands, depending on thickness of yarn. Instructions for hair are for hand sewing. Glue can be used instead, or a combination of sewing and glue.
Sash and Hair Bows can be made with bias tape or ribbon, rather than cut and sewn.
Trim can be flat or gathered lace.
Snaps can be plastic or metal or replaced by buttons.

COPYRIGHT and CHILD SAFETY

COPYRIGHT

What **CAN** you do? You **CAN** sell the items that you make from this pattern. You can use the templates to create the doll. You can also add your own artistic flare to what you create when using the templates. What you make is your property and is yours to do with as you wish.

What **CAN'T** you do? You **CANNOT** copy the pattern illustrations, diagrams, written instructions or photos. You cannot simply photocopy, scan, or reproduce the sewing pattern in any way and then sell copies of it. This is an infringement of copyright laws.

CHILD SAFETY

This doll is advised for children 3 years or older. For a younger child or baby, bows, sashes, ribbons, or any loose parts should be removed or sewn securely onto the doll or clothing. Fancy laces can wear out with use and separate from the clothing. They are preferable for children over 3. Plastic baby snaps can be used instead of metal snaps. The pattern calls for painting the face. Embroidery and painting are safety measures. Buttons should not be used for eyes for small children. I cannot be responsible for the way each crafter uses these patterns or instructions. Please consider the age of the child for which you are making the doll.

For more information on copyright laws and safety information, there is a great amount of information on the internet. For pattern questions, please send an email to Anne at this address: bluedaisyzone@gmail.com

Website: bluedaisyzone.com

Making the Doll

All seam allowances are 1/4 inch.
Use a small machine stich for more stability.

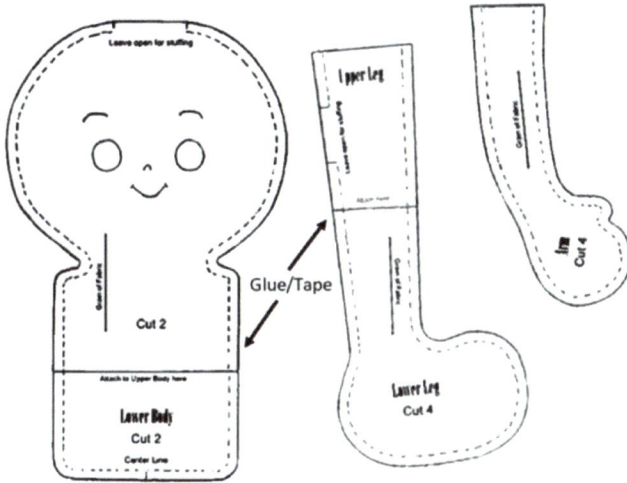

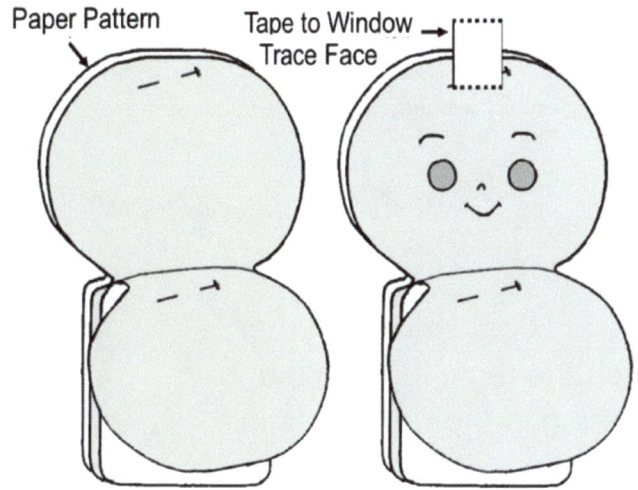

Cut out the patterns. Glue or tape the leg and body pieces together where indicated. Pin to fabric and cut out pieces.

FACE: Lay the fabric head/body on top of the paper pattern. Pin one side of the fabric head to the pattern top. Pin the folded layer of fabric to the lower body. Tape or hold the head/body to a window or lightbox and trace the face with pencil.

All the features can be painted or embroidered. I use acrylic paint for the eyes and Sharpie Permanent Markers for the nose, mouth, brows, and eyelashes. Don't forget to add a white dot to the eyes.

Marigold's eyes are dark green. I mixed a dot of black with shamrock green for the darker green. The lashes are black. The brows are brown. The nose and mouth are red. An orange/red blush from powdered makeup or pastel sticks for her cheeks will work well with Marigold's red hair and green eyes.

Leave Open

Clip

Reinforce
Curve

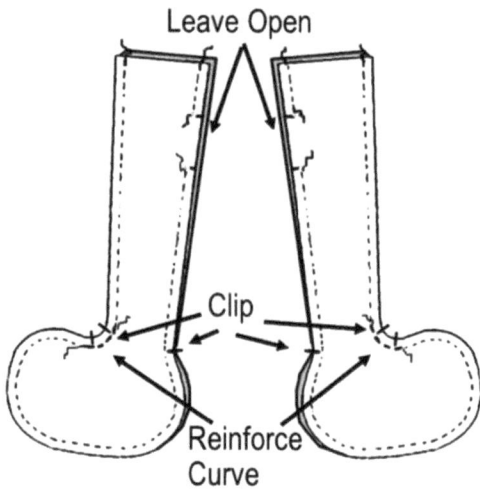

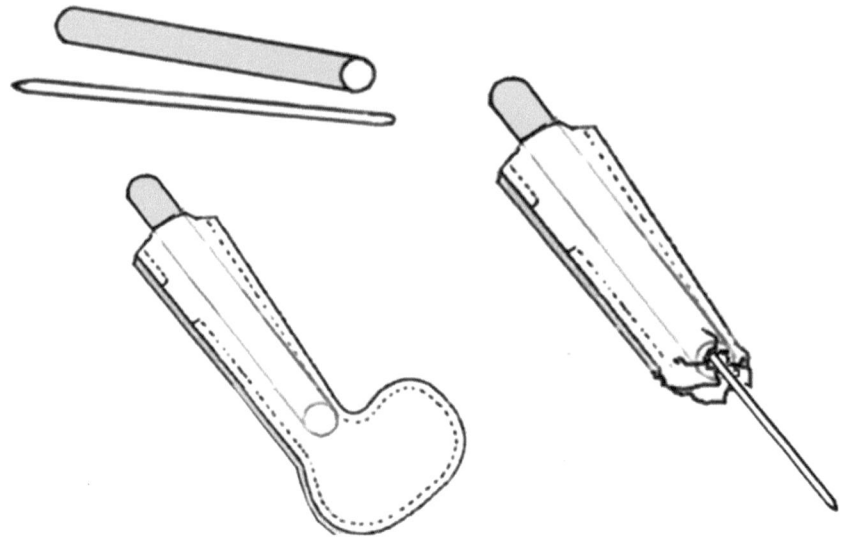

LEGS: Right sides together, stitch the legs, leaving the opening in the upper section for stuffing. Reinforce the curve between the top of the foot and leg. Clip curves.

Turn the legs right side out. My favorite way of turning narrow fabric pieces is with a tube and stick. In this case, push the tube inside the leg. With the stick, push the foot into the tube until it comes out the other end.

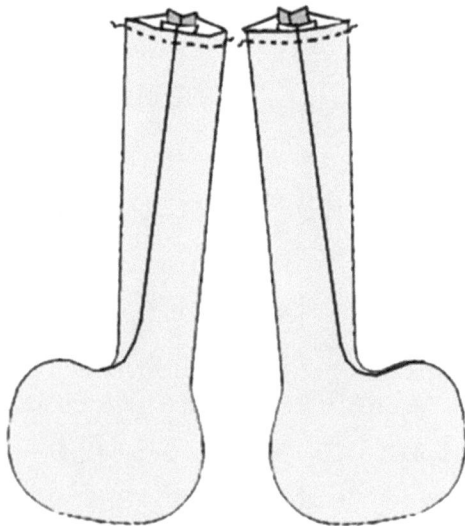

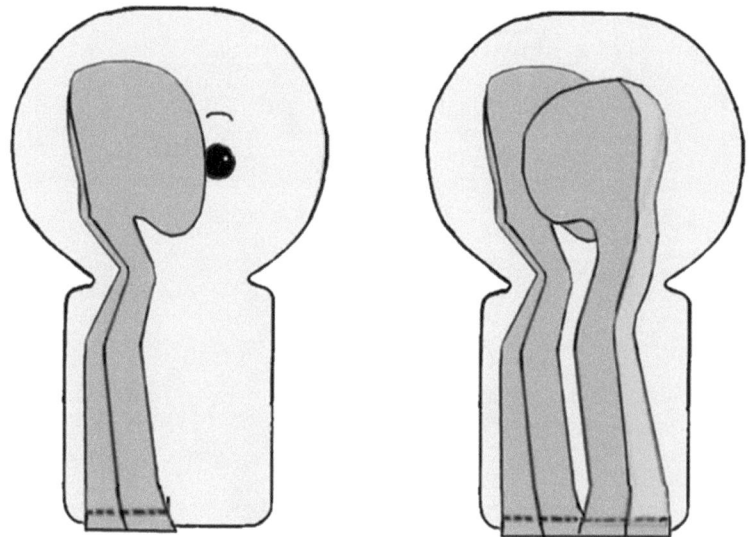

Open the top of the legs and pin the seams together. Baste across the top.

Place the top of the legs on the bottom of the right side of the body with the face. It's very important that the toes face the features on the face. Otherwise, the feet and legs will come out backwards. The leg tops should lie 1/4 inch from the side of the body on both sides. The legs should hang just below the body about 1/8 inch to make sure they are caught in the stitches. The legs might overlap a little in the middle. Pin/baste the legs in place along the bottom of the body.

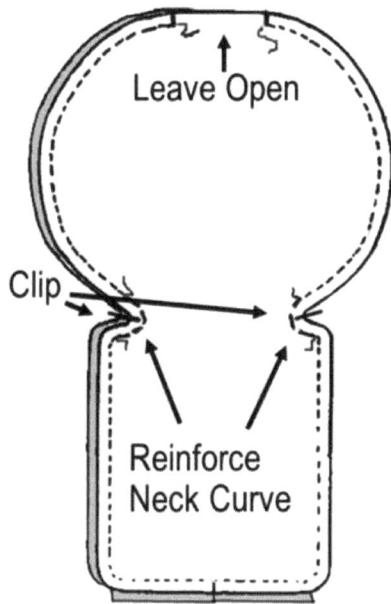

BODY: Right sides together, pin/baste the entire body, making sure the feet and legs are not caught in the seam allowance. Starting at the head, stitch around the entire body, leaving the opening for the stuffing. Reinforce the neck area with extra stitches. Clip the curves.

Turn the body right side out. Stuff the body and head. Sew the head closed with a ladder stitch as shown above.

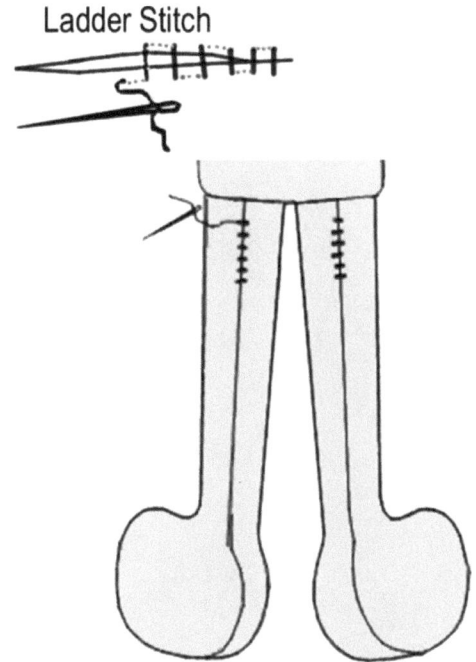

On the back side, stuff the legs. Close the legs with a ladder stitch.

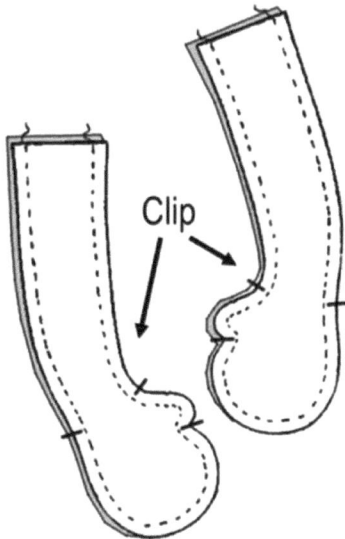

ARMS: Right sides together, stitch the arms. Clip curves. Turn right side out.

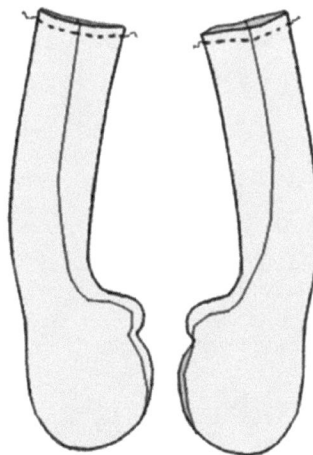

Stuff the arms to about 1 inch from the top. Turn the top edge inside 1/4 inch and pin closed. Hand sew or machine stitch closed.

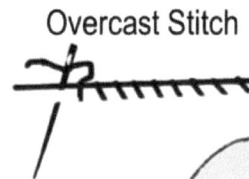

Pin arms to shoulders. Stitch by hand with an overcast stitch.

Making the Hair

Please read all the instructions before starting the hair.

Insert Yarn into Slits

Wrap Loosely

2. Insert the beginning end of the yarn into the slits with the line of yarn facing forward. Begin loosely wrapping yarn around the cardboard 33 times, covering the 7-inch line.

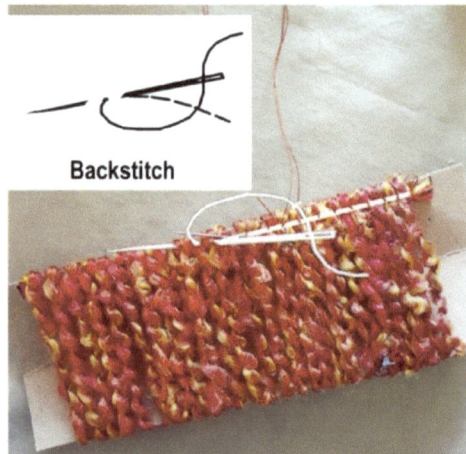

Make 1/4" Cut into Cardboard

7"

1. BANGS: For the curly bangs, lightweight cardboard that can bend easily will facilitate the removal of the yarn after it is wrapped. Make the cardboard 8"x3". Mark a line 7 inches long across the top edge. Cut a 1/4 inch slit into the cardboard at each end of the 7-inch mark.

Backstitch

3. With strong matching thread or yarn, use backstitch to sew the strands together, catching the 7-inch strand underneath.

Fold Cardboard Gently Slip Off Yarn

4. Bend the cardboard inward and carefully slip the yarn off in one piece.

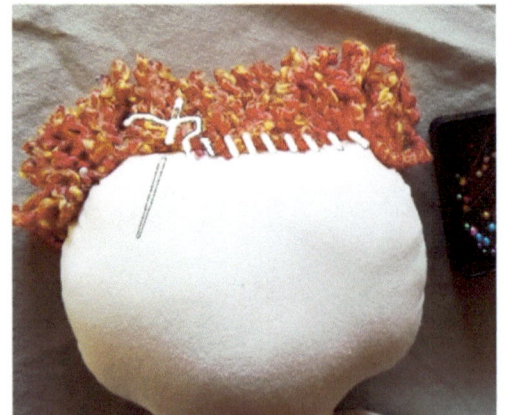

Center and Pin

5. Place the sewn yarn line toward the back and center bangs on head just in front of seam line. Pin in place. Use an overcast stitch to sew from end to end. Trim any loose strands of yarn on the ends.

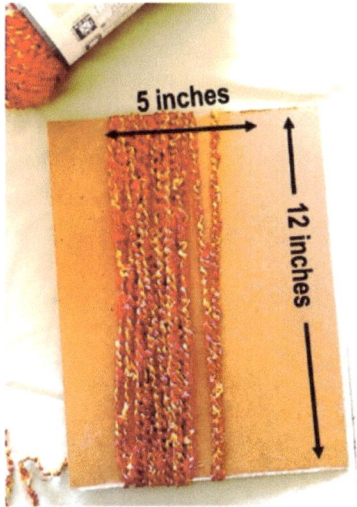

6. HAIR: Use a 12-inch piece of solid cardboard and wrap the yarn 60 times around the 12-inch side. Cover 5 inches across the top.

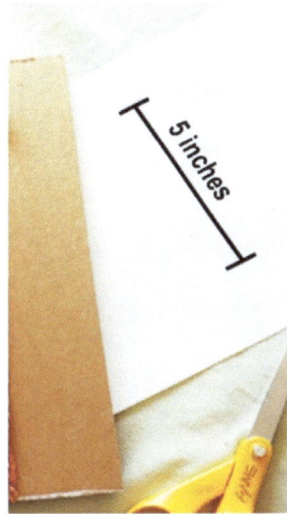

7. Prepare a piece of copy paper or stabilizer material at least 8"x7" to hold yarn during sewing. Draw a 5-inch line down the middle.

8. Place a piece of masking tape about an inch down from the top of the yarn and let it overlap onto the cardboard. Do this on both sides at the top. This will temporarily hold the yarn strands together. Clip the yarn at the opposite end.

9. For easier handling, loosely tie a string or piece of yarn half-way up each side. Carefully move the yarn from the cardboard and center it across the 5-inch line on the paper. Press down the tape to hold it in place on both sides of the paper.

10. Using a small stitch, sew the yarn on the paper, centering the stitches between the pieces of tape. A small stitch will make the perforations in the paper easier to tear away later.

Backstitch Part

Overstitch on top of Bangs

11. Remove the tape and tear away the paper. The seam forms the part for the back of the head.

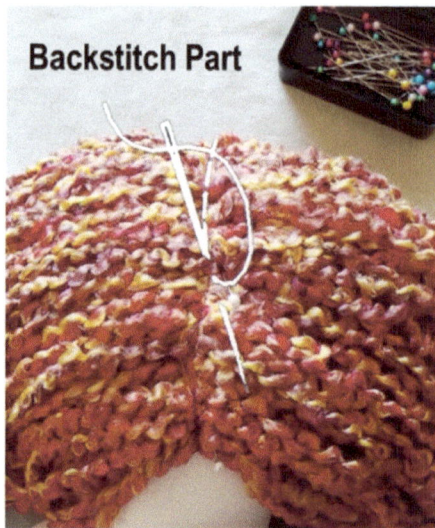

12. Center the yarn on the back of the doll's head. Line up the top of the yarn at the bangs. Pin and sew the part into place with a backstitch. Sew several strands across the bangs and down the side of the face 1/4 inch in front of the head seam.

13. Remove the string holding the strands together. Twist the yarn toward the front of the face. It helps to use some kind of clip or weight to hold the twist in place, but not necessary. Place a long strand of yarn under the hair at the jawline. Tie the strand tightly into a knot close to the face. Repeat for the other side. Trim the ends of the hair to the desired length.

Making the Clothes

All seam allowances are 1/4 inch.

Cut out paper pattern and glue/tape Skirt Front to Skirt Back. Cut out the fabric.

All edges can be finished by using an overstitch or making a tiny fold inward on the edge of the fabric. I use a pinking shears to cut out my pattern pieces and leave this as my finished edge.

Bloomers

Fold up lower edge of bloomers 1/4 inch. Press.

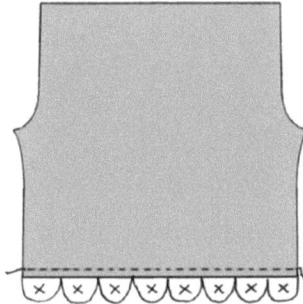

Pin/baste trim to lower edge and stitch. You can attach the trim on either side of the fabric, depending on your preference or on the finished edge of the trim.

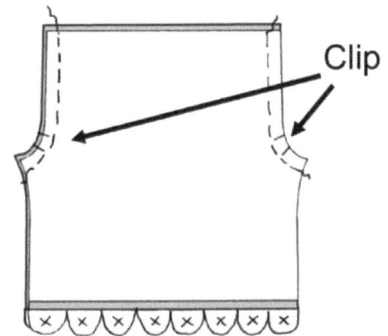

With right sides together, stitch the crotch seams. Clip curves.

Right sides together, stitch leg seams. Clip curves near crotch. Press seam open.

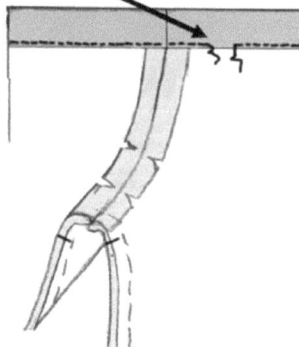

Fold top edge over 1/4 inch then another 1/2 inch to form casing for elastic. Press. Stitch near lower edge. Leave a section open for inserting elastic.

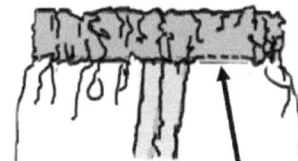

Insert Elastic on Safety Pin

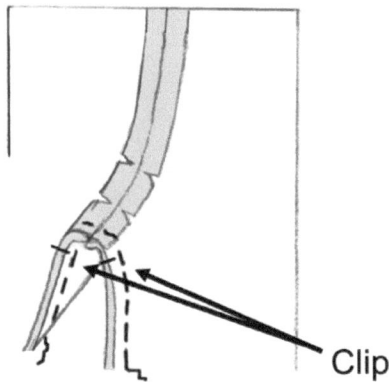

Stitch closed

Cut 9 inches of elastic. Insert into the casing on a safety pin. Push pin through to the other side. Overlap the elastic 1/4 inch. Stitch elastic together securely. By hand or machine, stitch the casing closed.

Dress

Clip

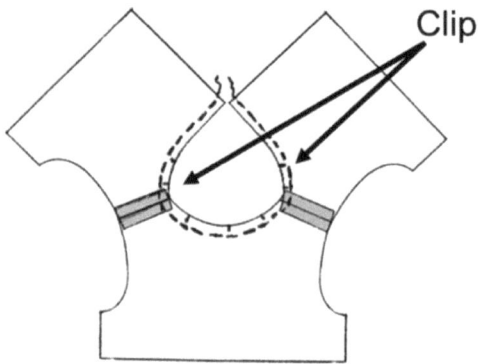

Right bodice sides together, stitch shoulder seams. Press open. Stay-stitch around neck to give it stability. Clip curves.

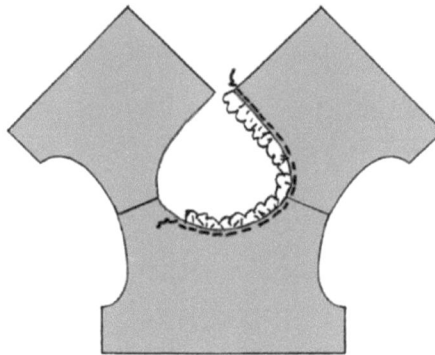

Press neck edge under at stay-stitching. Pin/baste trim to neck and stitch. Trim can be sewn on inside or outside of fabric, depending on preference or on the finished edge of the trim.

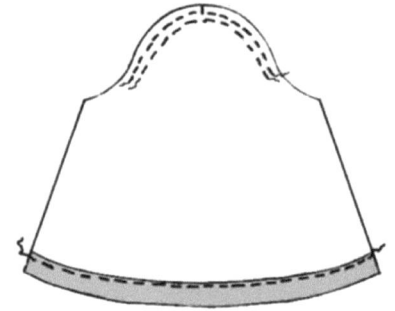

Make two rows of running stitches at the top of the sleeve for gathering. Press the lower edge under 1/4 inch then another 1/2 inch to form elastic casing. Stitch close to edge of casing.

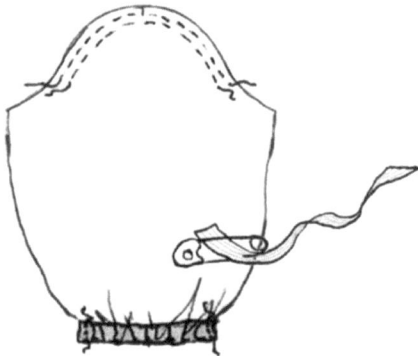

Insert a 4-inch piece of elastic on a safety pin into one end of the sleeve casing. Push the pin through the casing until about 1/8 inch of elastic is exposed. Stitch to hold elastic in place. Push pin through casing to other end. Remove pin. Leave about 1/8 inch outside casing. Stitch in place.

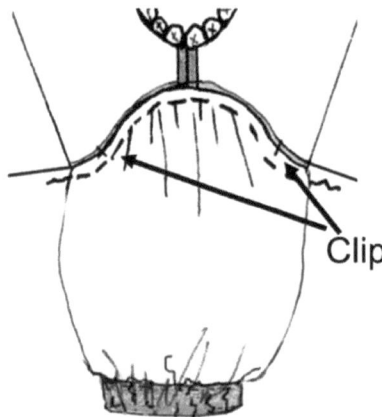

Clip

Right sides together, match center of sleeve to the shoulder seam. Pull up gathering threads to fit armhole. Pin/baste sleeve to armhole and stitch. Clip curves.

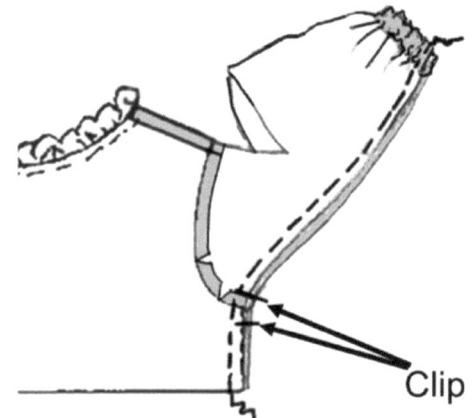

Clip

Fold armhole seam toward sleeve. Pin/baste and stitch the underarm seams from bodice to end of sleeve. Clip curves near armhole seams.

Mark half and quarters

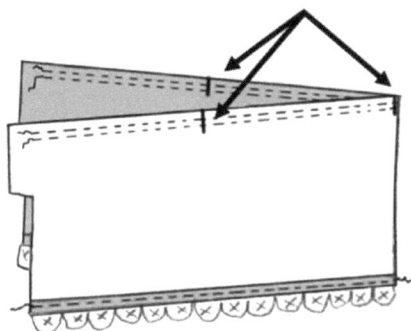

Clip

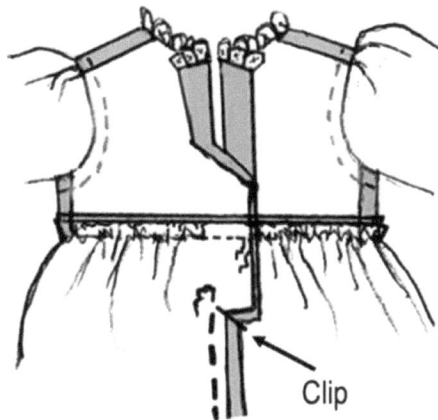

At top of skirt, mark the half-fold and quarter sections for matching bodice. Make two rows of running stitches for gathers from the facing fold line to facing fold line. Press up bottom edge 1/4 inch. Attach trim and stitch in place.

Pin/baste skirt to bodice, matching quarter marks to side seams and half-mark to center of bodice. Pull up gathering threads to fit. Stitch waist. Stitch back seam from bottom of skirt to about 1 inch up into the facing. Clip at facing.

Press facing toward wrong side of fabric. Stitch facing edge from collar to clipped seam.

Leave Open

Clip Corners

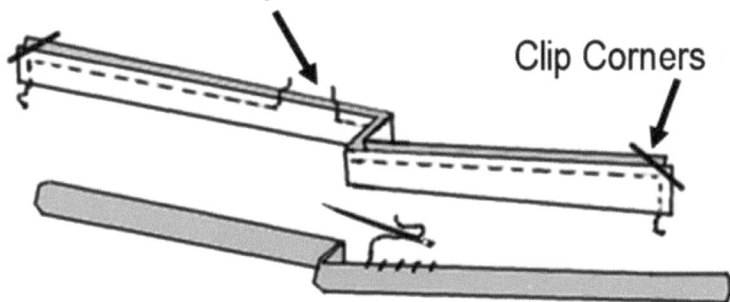

Waist Line

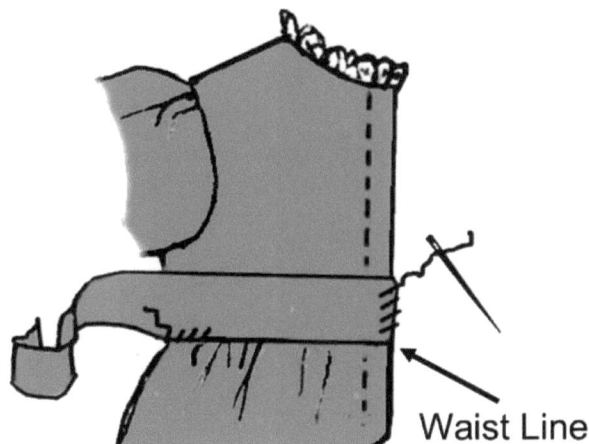

The sash is formed by two ties that come together in the front of the bodice to form a bow. Cut two pieces of fabric 16"x2". Fold each piece in half longwise. Pin and stitch, starting from each end and leaving about a 1-inch opening near the middle. Trim ends and turn right side out. Close the open section with an overcast stitch.

On each side of the back, line up a sash tie with the waist line at the facing. Pin the ribbon in place and hand stitch along outer edge with an overcast stitch. Make a few overcast stitches at the side seams to hold the ties in place.

BACK

FRONT

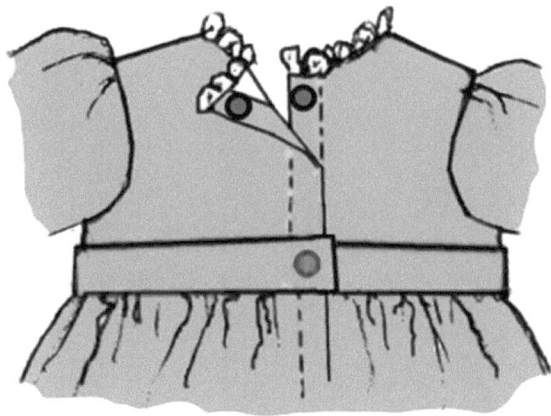

On the back side, overlap the left side on top of the right side. Attach snaps to top of bodice and at waist.

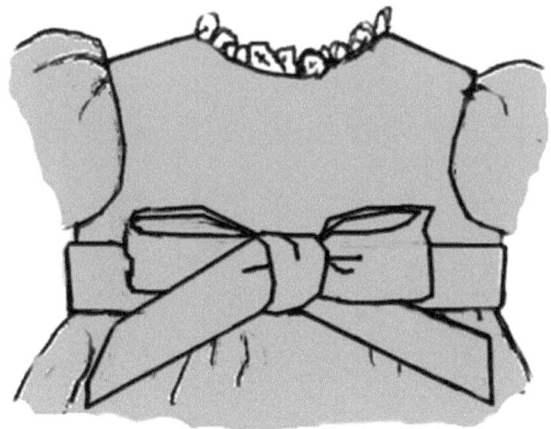

On the front side, bring the sash ties together at the center or asymmetrically to the left side and tie into a neat bow. Tack in place.

Hair Bows

Leave Open

Clip Corners

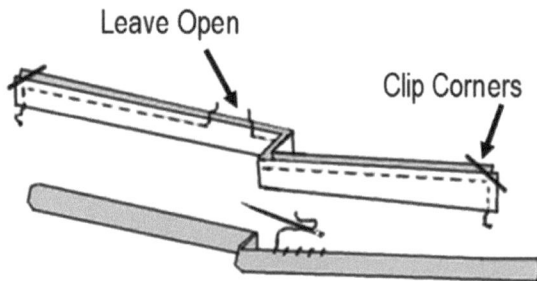

For hair bows, cut two pieces of fabric 20"x2". Fold in half longwise and follow the instructions for the sash. Tie a neat bow on each of Marigold's pigtails.

Shoes

Reinforce

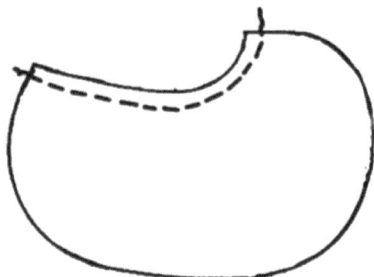

On each shoe piece, stay-stitch along top edge for stability.

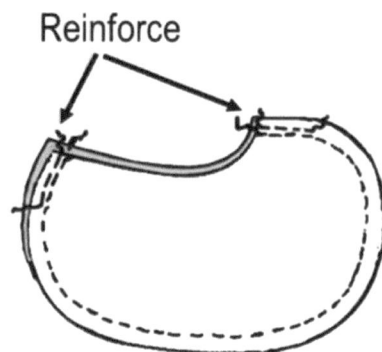

With right sides together, stitch from toe to back of heel. Reinforce beginning and ending with extra stitches for stability.

Patterns
For
Doll and Clothing

Patterns can be cut out or traced.

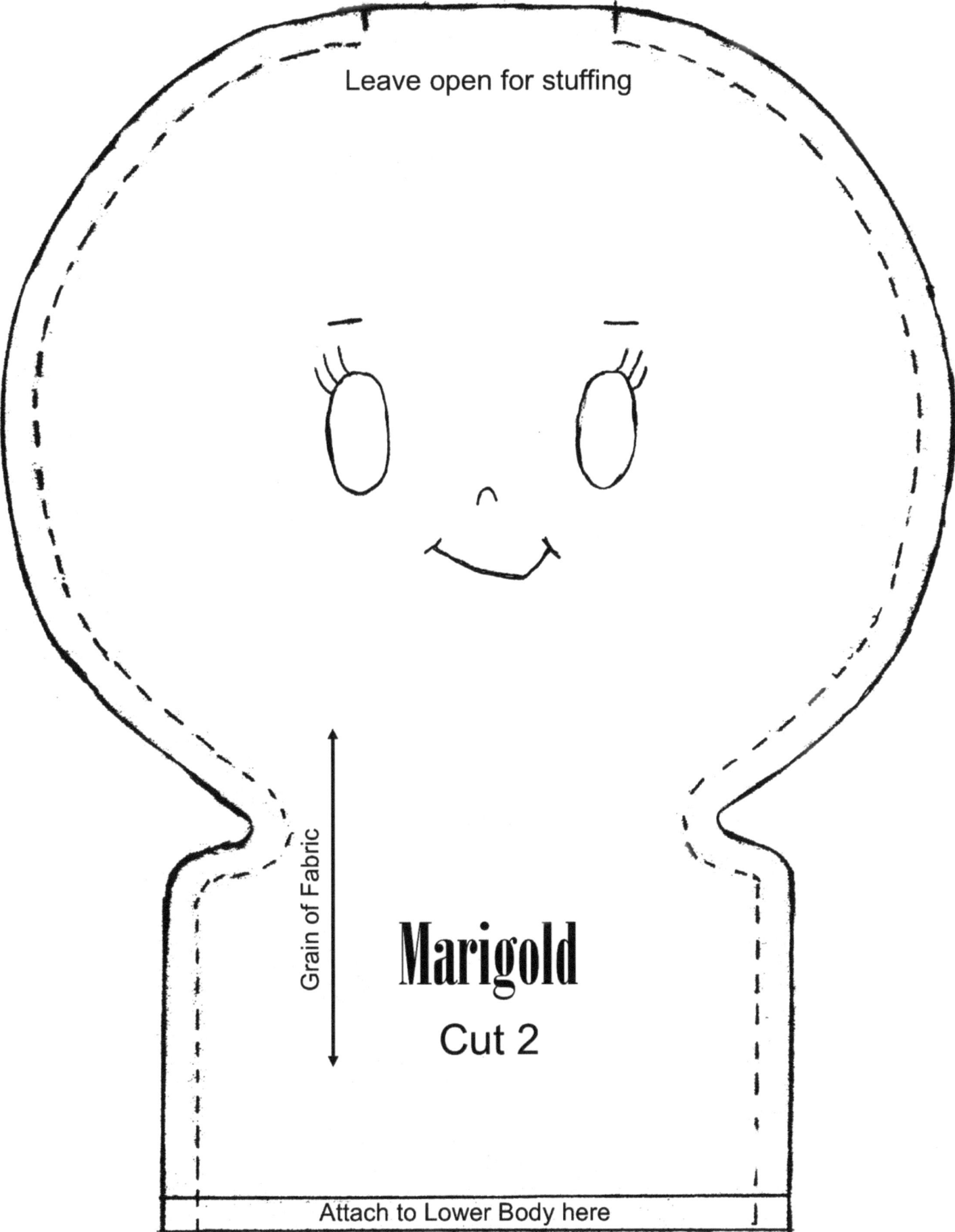

Leave open for stuffing

Grain of Fabric

Marigold

Cut 2

Attach to Lower Body here

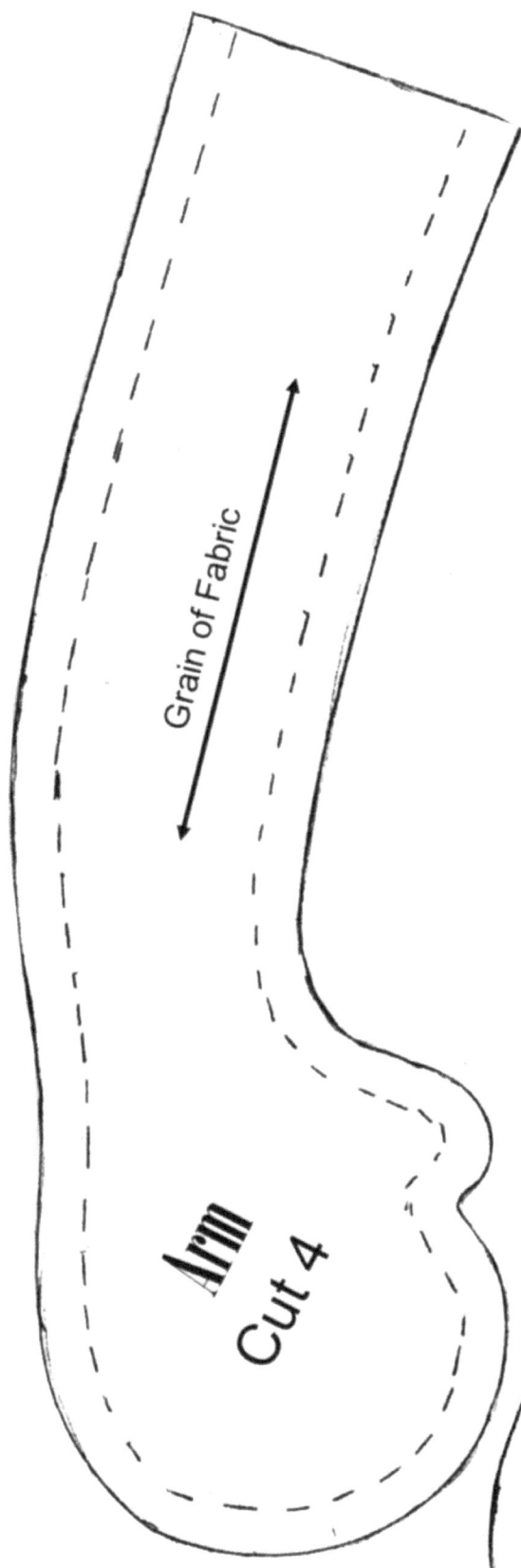

Grain of Fabric

Arm
Cut 4

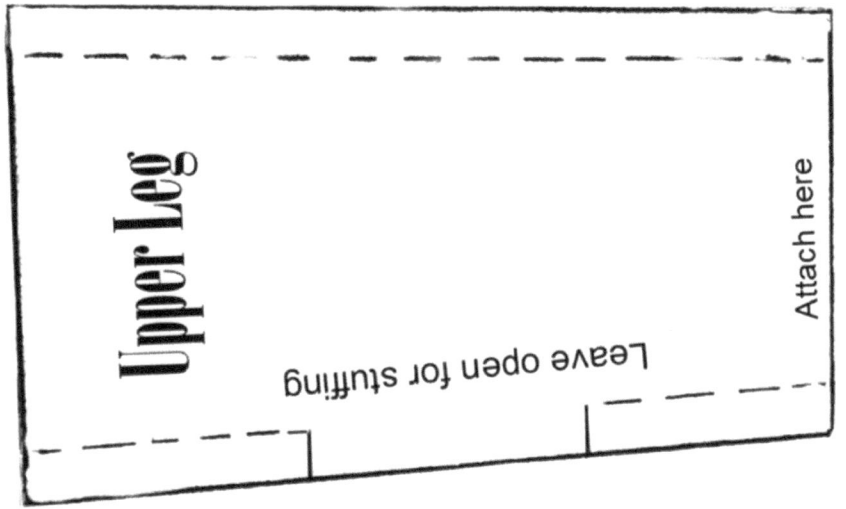

Upper Leg

Attach here

Leave open for stuffing

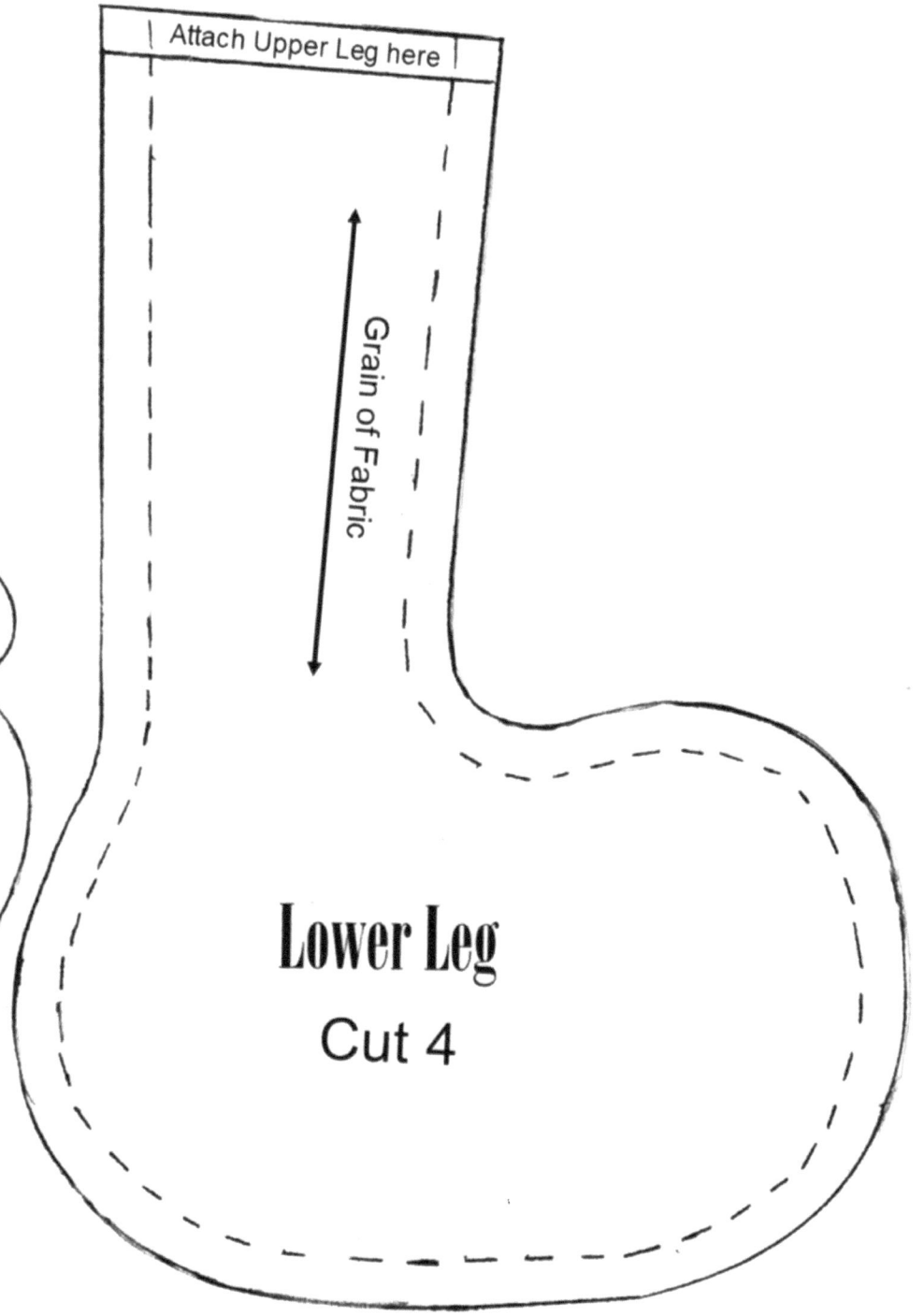

Attach Upper Leg here

Grain of Fabric

Lower Leg

Cut 4

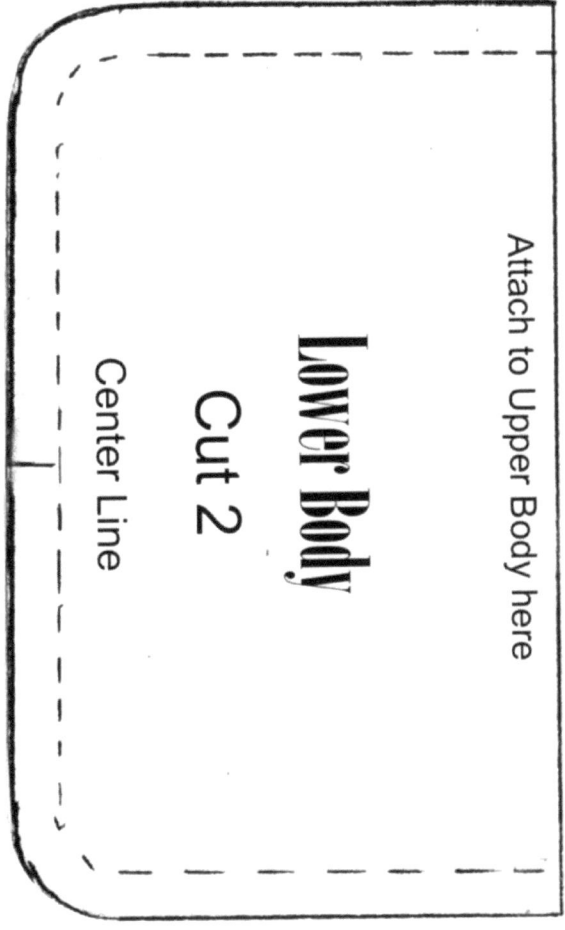

Attach to Upper Body here

Lower Body
Cut 2

Center Line

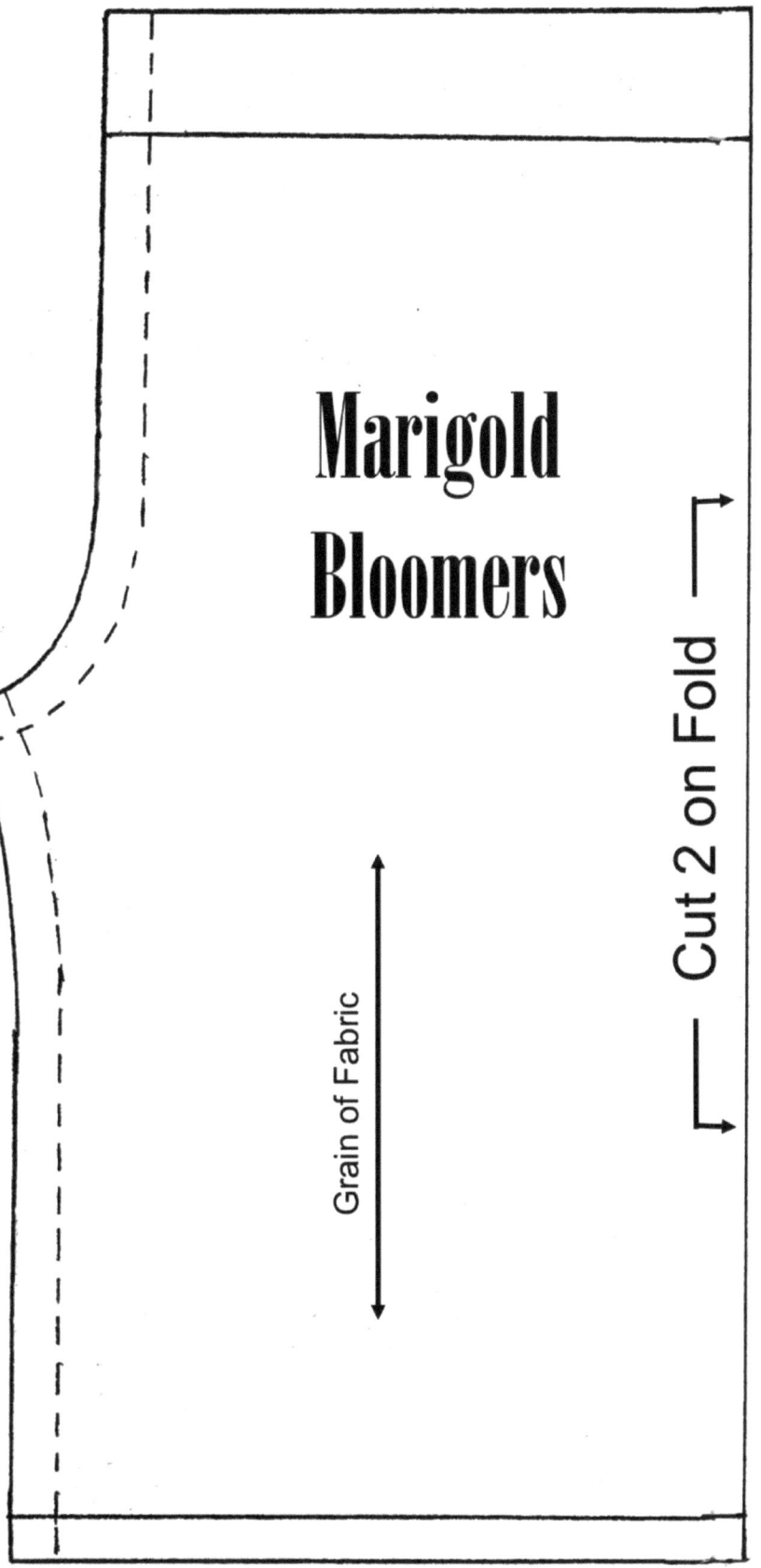

Marigold Bloomers

Grain of Fabric

Cut 2 on Fold

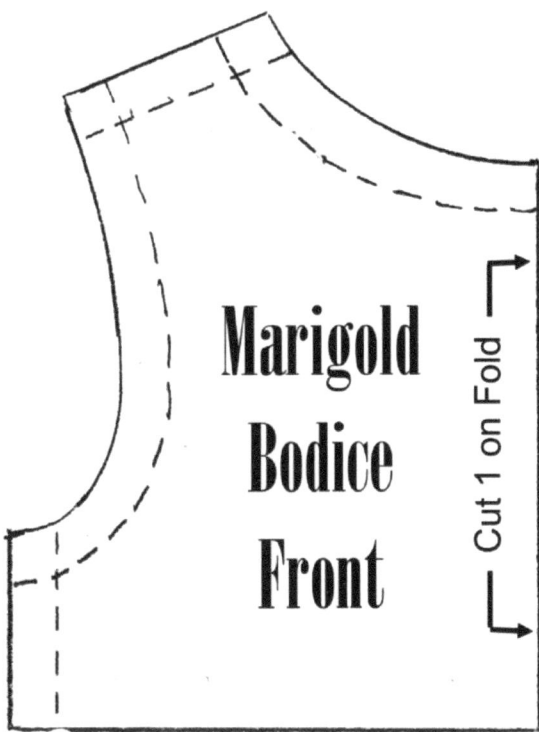

Marigold
Bodice
Front

Cut 1 on Fold

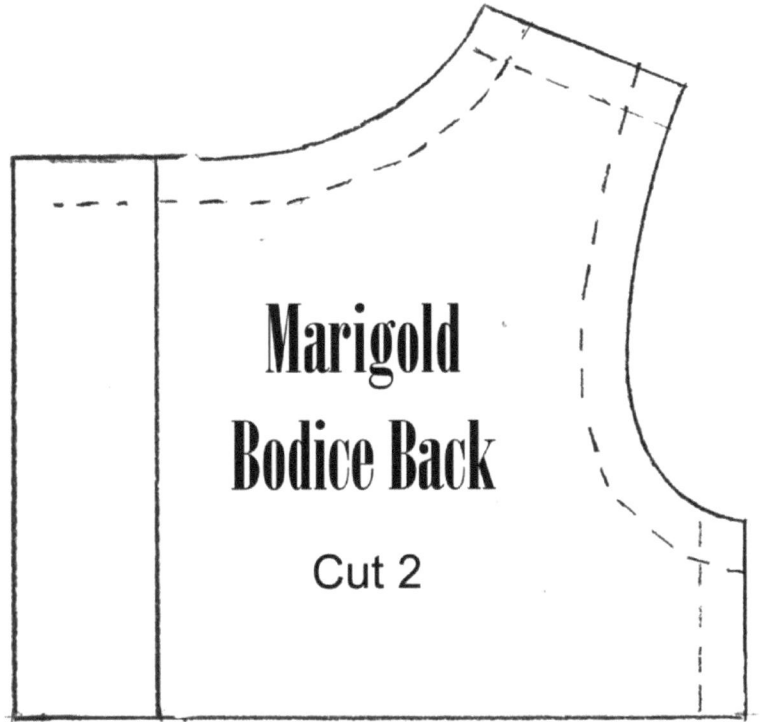

Marigold
Bodice Back

Cut 2

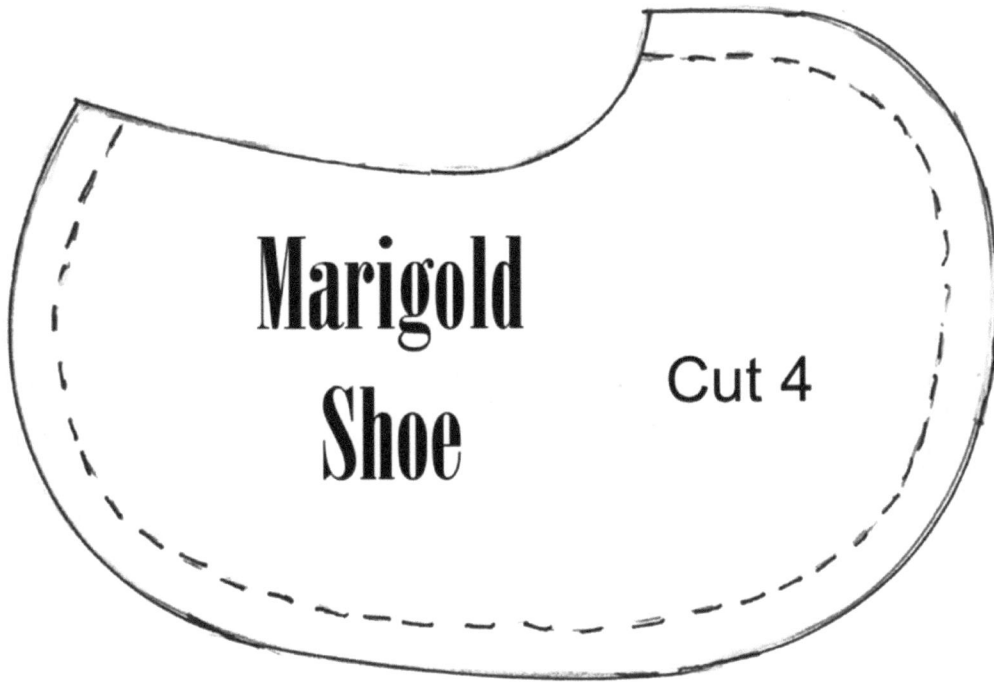

Marigold
Shoe

Cut 4

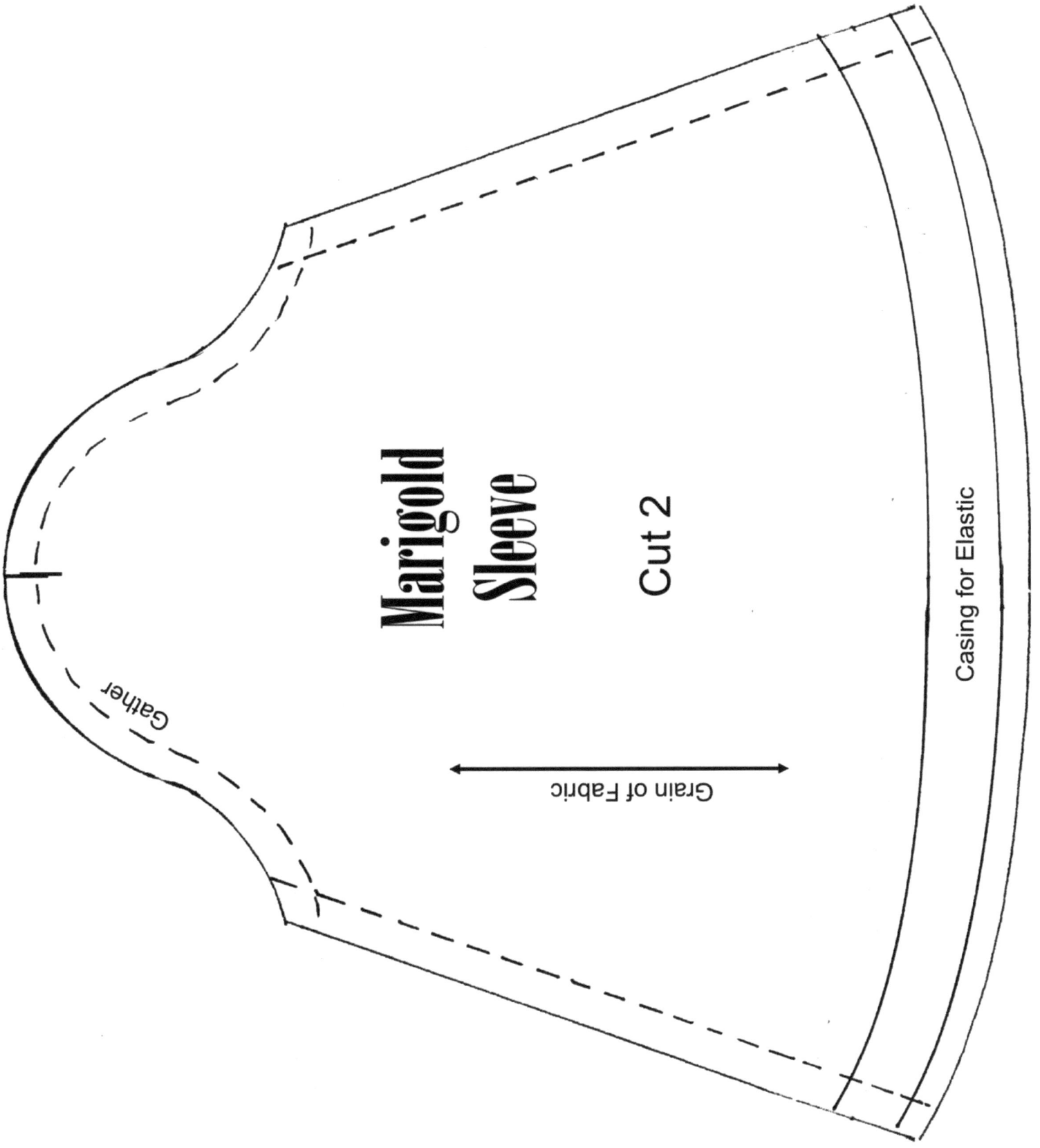

Marigold Sleeve

Cut 2

Gather

Gather

Grain of Fabric

Casing for Elastic

Gather for Waist

Marigold
Dress Front

Attach to Dress Back here

Cut 1 on Fold

Marigold
Dress Back

Attach to Dress Front here